Know About
Taj Mahal

Contents

Preface

The Taj Mahal, mausoleum of the Mughal Empress Mumtaz Mahal, the world looks upon this spectacular structure with amaze. The Taj is undoubtedly one of the most magnificent buildings of the world. An outstanding example of Mughal architecture which combined Persian, Indian and Islamic art and cultural influences. Due to its aesthetic beauty, the Taj Mahal still remains one of the most celebrated and visited structure of the world. It was designated a UNESCO World Heritage site in 1983. It counts among man's proudest creations and is invariably included in the list of the world's foremost wonders.

As a tomb, it has no match upon earth, for mortal remains have never been housed in greater grandeur.

CHAPTER 1
History of Taj Mahal

In 1612, Arjumand Banu Begum, better known by her other name, Mumtaz Mahal was married to Shah Jahan (then Prince Khurram), the fifth Mughal Emperor. This

marriage, although the emperor's second, was a real love-match and Mumtaz was her husband's inseparable companion on all his journeys and military expeditions. She was his comrade, his counsellor and inspired him to acts of charity and benevolence towards the weak and the needy. She bore him fourteen children and died in childbed in 1631(only three years after his accession to the throne) in Burhanpur in the Deccan where she had accompanied him on a military campaign. Overpowered by grief, Shah Jahan was determined to perpetuate her memory for immortality and decided to build his beloved wife the finest sepulchre ever - a monument of eternal love. It was Shah Jahan's everlasting love for Mumtaz that led to the genesis of the Taj Mahal. The sad circumstances which attended the early death of the Empress who had endeared herself to the people inspired all his subjects to join in the emperor's pious intentions. After twenty-two laborious

years and the combined effort of over twenty thousand workmen and master craftsmen, the complex was finally completed in 1648 on the banks of river Yamuna in Agra, the capital of Mughal monarchs.

The origin of the name the 'Taj Mahal' is not clear. Court histories from Shah Jahan's reign only call it the 'rauza' (tomb) of Mumtaz Mahal. It is generally believed that 'Taj Mahal' (usually translated as either 'Crown Palace' or 'Crown of the Palace') is an abbreviated version of her name, Mumtaz Mahal (Exalted One of the Palace).

CHAPTER 2
The Architecture of The Taj

Darwaza - The gate way map

Shah Jahan travelled from the fort to the tomb by boat. Court histories describe his arrival on the river side of the monument and his ascent to its terrace by way of the embankment. This approach, however, was reserved for the Emperor and members of his party. Others passed through a large courtyard, Jilokhana to enter the main

gateway on the south. This courtyard was a place where travellers halted. Here, also, the poor were provided with food and shelter and on the anniversary day vast sums were distributed in charity from the funds with which the Taj was endowed.

Reason

In this courtyard stand the main gateway to the Taj and its gardens, a massive portal that opens to the south. Detached gateways were a long traditional feature of Muslim architecture and could be found fronting tombs and mosques throughout the East. Symbolically to the Muslim, such an entrance way was the gate to paradise. Metaphysically, it represented the transition point between the outer world of the senses and the inner world of the spirit.

Structure

Made of red sandstone, this 150 ft. wide and nearly 100 ft. high, gateway consists of a lofty central arch with double-storeyed wings on either side. Octagonal towers are attached to its corners which are surmounted by broad impressive open domed kiosks. The most important feature of the gateway however is the introduction of a series of eleven attached 'chhatris' (umbrellas) with marble cupolas, flanked by pinnacles, above the central portal on the north and south sides. A heavy door at the base is made from eight different metals and studded with knobs. Inside are countless rooms with hallways that wind and divide in such apparent abandon that they seem intentionally built to confuse; perhaps they were, for they have remained unused for three centuries and their purpose has long confounded the experts. Within the archway of this majestic entrance, there is a large chamber with a vaulted roof.

Decoration

The gateway is richly embellished. Of particular note are the floral arabesques fashioned from gemstones and inlaid in white marble which decorate the spandrels of the arches. Also impressive are the inlaid black marble inscriptions that frame the central vaulted portal or iwan.

These passages are excerpts from the Quran, which is considered by Muslims to be the word of God as revealed to Mohammed. It is here that Shah Jahan's calligraphers have performed an amazing optical trick: the size of the lettering that runs up and over the arch appears to be consistent from top to bottom. This illusion was created by gradually heightening the size of the letters as their distance from the eye increased; from the ground the dimensions seem the same at every point. This ingenious *trompe l'oeil* effect is used with equal success on the main doorway of the Taj itself.

It is said that upon first beholding the Taj through this gateway it will look small and far away, as if built in three-quarter scale. This is another optical trick. As one approaches, the illusion turns into another illusion: the building begins to grow and continues to grow until, when the base is reached, it looms colossal. The dome especially seems to expand as one comes near, almost as if it were being slowly inflated.

CHAPTER 3
Bageecha - The Taj Gardens

The Gardens

A green carpet of garden runs from the main gateway to the foot of the Taj. This garden which beautifies the Taj is Persian Timurid Style of gardens and is based on the concept of Paradise Garden. Such gardens were introduced to India by Babur, the first Mughal Emperor, who also brought with him the Persian infatuation with flowers and fruit, birds and leaves, symmetry and delicacy.

Unlike other Oriental gardens - especially those of the Japanese, who learned to accentuate existing resources rather than formalize them - the Persian garden was artificially contrived, unabashedly man-made, based on geometric arrangements of nature without any attempt at a 'natural' look.

Like Persian gardeners, landscape artists at the Taj attempted to translate the perfection of heaven into terrestrial terms by following certain formulas. In Islam, four is the holiest of all numbers - most arrangements of the Taj are based on the number four or its multiples - and the gardens were thus laid out in the quadrate plan. Two marble canals studded with fountains and lined with cypress trees (symbolising death) cross in the centre of the garden dividing it into four equal squares. The mausoleum, instead of occupying the central point (like

most Mughal mausoleums) stands majestically at the north end just above the river. Each of the four quarters of the garden has again been sub-divided into sixteen flower beds by stone-paved raised pathways. At the centre of the garden, halfway between the tomb and the gateway, stands a raised marble lotus-tank with a cusped and tre-foiled border. The tank has been arranged to perfectly reflect the Taj in its waters.

A clear, unobstructed view of the mausoleum is available from any spot in the garden. Fountains and solemn rows of cypress trees only adorn the north-south water canal, lest the attention of the viewer would be diverted to the sides. This shows how carefully the aesthetic effect of the water devices and the garden were calculated. The deep green cypress trees with their slender rising shapes and curving top most crests are mirrored in the water while between their dark reflections shines the beauty of the immortal Taj.

CHAPTER 4
The Water Devices

The architect, who was fully aware of the unaesthetic appearance of the grotesque pur-ramps and crude conduits, designed a clever system to procure water for the Taj through underground pipes.

Water was drawn from the river by a series of purs (manual system of drawing water from a water body using a rope and bucket pulled by bullocks) and was

brought through a broad water channel into an oblong storage tank of great dimensions. It was again raised by a series of thirteen purs worked by bullocks. Except for the ramps, the other features of the whole water system have survived. An over-head water-channel supported on massive arches carried water into another storage tank of still greater dimensions. Water was finally raised by means of fourteen purs and passed into a channel which filled three supply tanks, the last of which had pipe mouths in its eastern wall. The pipes descended below and after travelling underground crossed into the Taj enclosure. One pipe line runs directly towards the mosque to supply the fountains in the tanks on the red sandstone plinth below the marble structure. Copper pipes were used for separate series of fountains in the north-south canal, lotus pond and the canal around it.

An ingenious method was devised to ensure uniform and undiminished water pressure in the fountains, irrespective of the distance and the outflow of water. The fountain pipes were not connected directly with the copper pipes feeding them as this would have resulted in a gradual decrease in the volume and pressure of the water. Instead, a copper pot has been provided under each fountain pipe - which was thus, connected to with the water supply only through the pot. Water first fills the pot and then only rises simultaneously in the fountains. The fountains are thus, controlled by pressure in the pots and not by the pressure in the main pipe. As the pressure in the pots is uniformly distributed all the time, it ensures equal supply of water at the same rate in all the fountains. It is really creditable that the planner spared no efforts - belonging to art, architecture and engineering -to create a perfect production without the slightest weakness, architectural or aesthetic. The main supply of the water was however obtained through earthenware pipes. One such main was discovered under the bed of the western canal. The pipe is 9" in diameter and has been embedded in masonry at a depth of 5 feet below the level of the paved walk. Evidently, the Mughal water expert was a master of his art and successfully worked out the levels in relation to the volume of water to ensure its unobstructed supply for centuries.

He anticipated no repair work and therefore made no provision fork; hence the extraordinary depth at which the pipe was sunk.

The garden is irrigated by the overflowing of canals. The north-south canal has inlets of water through fountains. The east-west received its water through an interconnection with the north-south canal. Thus the quarters near the canals received an adequate supply of water and could be used for growing flower-plants which would not obscure the general view, while the distant quarters got a smaller supply of water and were suitable only for tall trees.

CHAPTER 5
Masjid - The Mosque

On either side of the Taj Mahal are buildings of red sandstone. The one to the west is a Mosque. It faces towards Mecca and is used for prayer. Before we have a look at the mosque, let us take note of a small stone enclosure along the western boundary wall where the well of the Mosque is located. This greenery shaded structure, measuring 19 ft. by 6.5 ft. marks the site where the remains of Mumtaz Mahal were deposited when first brought to Agra. From this temporary grave they were removed to their present place of internment in the mausoleum.

On the outside the Mosque is the pietra dura work twining across its spandrels. The platform in front of the Mosque is of red sandstone. A highly polished small marble piece is so fitted that it serves as a mirror and one can see the mausoleum reflected in it. The floor is of material which is exceedingly fine and sparkling and appears velvet red in shade. On that 539 prayer carpets have been neatly marked out with black marble. All over there is exquisite calligraphy and the name Allah and quotations from scriptures inscribed. The ceiling is painted in a strange, hypnotic design. The roof supports four octagonal towers and three elegant domes. On either side of the Mosque, to the north and south and set along and upon the enclosure wall, there are two towers.

CHAPTER 6
Naqqar Khana -The Rest House

On the east side of the Taj stands the twin of the Mosque, a parallel structure also made of red sandstone, referred to as the jawab, or 'answer'. Because it faced away from the Mecca, it was never used for prayer. Its presence there has always been something of an enigma. Was it a caravanserai for pilgrims, or a meeting hall before the faithful gathered for prayer? More plausible is the theory that its purpose

was purely architectural, to counter balance the Mosque and preserve the symmetry of the entire design on the platform.

The jawab is similar to the Mosque. However, it does not contain the accessories which go with a mosque and, instead of Quranic inscriptions; there are beautiful flower designs and other decoration effectively done in white marble on the red sandstone background. On the floor between the building and the mausoleum there is a full size reproduction of the pinnacle adorning the Taj. This gives some idea of the true proportions (31 ft.) of what from below appears to be a tiny thing.

CHAPTER 7
Rauza - The Actual Tomb

The Taj Mahal is situated more than 900 ft. (275 m.) away from the entrance at the opposite end of the garden. Towering almost 240 ft. (73 m.) in height, the tomb stands on its own marble plinth, which rests on a red sandstone platform that serves to level the land as it slopes to the river. Four tall minarets rise up from the corners of the white marble plinth. They taper to a majestic height of

138 ft. and are crowned with eight windowed cupolas which elegantly accent the central structure, framing the space like the mounting of a jewel.

The marble mausoleum is square in plan with chamfered corners. Each facade of the tomb is composed of a grand iwan framed by bands of calligraphy. The doorways inside these iwans are also adorned with calligraphy. The iwan is flanked on both sides by small double arches one over the other. They are rectangular while the arched alcoves of equal size at the angles of the tomb are semi-octagonal. Each section in the facade is well demarked on both sides by attached pilasters which rising from the plinth level of the tomb rise above the frieze and are crowned by beautiful pinnacles with lotus buds and finials. The pinnacles ornament the superstructure and help along with the other features to break the skyline gracefully.

CHAPTER 8
Ornamentation of The Tomb

The domed mausoleum can seem deceptively simple since on first sight its white marble form appears to be a matchless example of purity and simplicity. But as one moves closer, the Taj Mahal's elaborate design reveals itself. While individual elements such as the refined inlays and myriad surface details are testimony to the fine quality of this monument, it is the superb manner in which all the elements are harmonised. And that most clearly reveals the great complexity of its creation. An often repeated nineteenth century characterization of the monument is that 'it was built by Titans, finished by Jewellers'.

The major modes of ornamentation found on the monument are:

- Pietra dura inlay
- Hardstone carving
- Calligraphy
- Incised paintings (in the mosque and its jawab)

The exterior of the Taj Mahal is a seemingly perfect

balance of ornamented and unadorned surfaces. The techniques of this decoration and the motifs used are characteristic not only of Shah Jahan's architectural projects, but also of the other arts that flourished during his reign. Intricate floral and geometric inlays, profuse surface detailing by reliefs and the exquisitely rendered calligraphic panels are all indicative of the great attention lavished on the building. Although geometric patterns appear, such as the ripple pattern inlaid in the terrace floor, floral designs are the dominant decorative motifs. As on the monumental gateway, inlays of floral arabesques embellish the spandrels of the arches, while elegant floral sprays sculpted in high relief appear on the dado of the exterior walls. Prominent calligraphic panels of black marble frame the iwans on each facade of the tomb.

The doorways inside these iwans are also adorned with calligraphy.

The Taj Mahal is entered through the portal on the south side. Inside, two stories of eight rooms (four rectangular rooms on the sides and four octagonal small rooms at the corners) surround a central chamber. These rooms were originally used for the mullahs to chant the Quran and for Musicians who played soft Indian and Persian melodies. In this nine part plan, the visitor can circumambulate through the subsidiary rooms on each floor since they are interconnected. The central chamber is octagonal and in the centre is the tomb of the queen and to one side is the casket of the emperor. The hall is 80 ft. high from the pavement to the soffit of the interior dome. This makes sound echo.

A bulbous white double-dome majestically crowns the Taj. The huge dome emphasises the monumentality of the structure as its pear shaped form sits on a tall drum. The height from the base of the drum to the top of the finial is almost 145 ft. (44 m.). The double domes fulfil various purposes. Besides providing a suitable and proportionate ceiling to the interior hall, it enabled the builder to raise the height of the outer dome as much as he desired in order to present a lofty and imposing effect. The space within the two domes is hollow and the inner cell reduces the weight of the dome. Four small kiosks clustered around the dome reduce the severity of the vertical emphasis.

CHAPTER 9
Pietra Dura Inlay

The technique known as pietra dura, whereby thin sections of precisely carved hard and semi hard gemstones are laid in sockets specially prepared in the surface of marble, is another mode of ornamentation prominently featured on the Taj Mahal. Here, the pietra dura inlay is wrought into the form of arabesque floral tendrils which meander over the surface of the white marble in a lyrical and graceful pattern that transcends its inherently restrictive symmetry.

The use of pietra dura in India has become a matter of great controversy for years. Some have claimed that it was derived from Florentine traditions, others that it developed independently in India. Recently, it has been cogently argued that the technique was indeed Italian in origin, but that it was modified by Indian traditions of craftsmanship. The argument hinges on the recognition of the difference between two related types of inlay. Although conventional stone inlay had been known in India for a long time (stages of indigenous development from the Ranpur temple to the tomb of Akbar are perfectly clear), the practice of

pietra dura, which involves inlaying stones of extreme hardness, has in every instance of its development been traced back to an Italian source and it is quite likely that European craftsmen taught it to the Mughal artists. There is no doubt that the Mughal sovereigns freely entertained artists from Europe.

Both stone inlay and hard stone inlay are found in the tomb of Itimad-ud-daula and his wife at Agra, built between 1622 and 1628. But it was in the earliest projects of Shah Jahan's reign that the pietra dura work was fully perfected and then adopted as an important means of decoration - perhaps the ideal one to be employed at the court of an emperor who would appreciate both the high level of skill entailed by the process and the jewel-like qualities realised in its finest products.

Flowers

Flowers have long been important in Islamic cultures, where they were generally seen as symbols of the divine realm. The Mughals had maintained a special interest in flowers since the days of Babur, who was an avid garden-builder. ShahJahan's father Jehangir had been quite fascinated with nature and his passion for flowers is well documented by his memoirs. Shah Jahan seems to have shared this interest. Jehangir seems to have been the catalyst in the introduction of naturalistic plants into Mughal paintings, which were inspired by engravings in European herbal books that had been brought into India by foreign visitors. But it was in the time of Shah Jahan that Indian artists refined such depictions, transforming them into the hallmark of the Mughal decorative style. The Taj Mahal reveals that the importance of floral motifs in an architectural context was established early in the emperor's reign.

CHAPTER 10
Hardstone Carving

A long tradition of hard stone carving existed in India and the Islamic courts of Iran and Central Asia. The Mughals incorporated this art form into their architectural programs and corpus of decorative objects in the early seventeenth century. Although the technique of carving white marble as a building material was first utilised during the reign of Jehangir and jade luxury items were fashioned even

earlier, it was not until the reign of Shah Jahan that hard stone carving achieved its full artistic expression.

The Taj Mahal displays exquisitely carved modelled floral sprays sculpted in shallow relief in white marble. The superb quality of the sculpted flowers on the mausoleum can be attributed to the ancient tradition of stone carving in India. These reliefs, however, are also indebted to European sources for their more naturalistic forms. Besides its architectural role, hard stone carving was also used to create decorative objects and vessels.

CHAPTER 11
Calligraphy

The inscriptions at the Taj Mahal have been judiciously selected and artistically inscribed over the main gateway, in the Mosque and the tomb proper, in panels around the arched portals, alcoves and the niches. They are chiefly verses from the Quran, which is considered by Muslims to be the word of God as revealed to Mohammed. While inlaying this calligraphy, Shah Jahan's calligraphers had

created an amazing optical trick: the size of the lettering that runs up and over the arch appears to be consistent from top to bottom. This illusion was created by gradually heightening the size of the letters as their distance from the eye increased; from the ground the dimensions seem the same at every point.

The South Gateway which is the main entrance, has along its front and sides, the whole chapter 'Walfazr' (The Daybreak) (Sura-89, containing 30 verses), chapter 'Wad-duha' (The Glorious Morning Light) (Sura-93, containing 11 verses), chapter "Wat-tin' (The Fig) (Sura-95, containing 8 verses) and chapter 'Alam-nashrah' (Have We Not Opened) (Sura-94, containing 8 verses).

Inside the Mosque have been inscribed fifteen verses of Sura-91, entitled 'Wash-Shams' (The Sun) and four of Sura-112 entitled 'Sura Ikhlas' (The Declaration of Gods Unity).

The portals (iwans) of the main tomb are adorned with the text of Sura-36 entitled 'Ya-Sin' (containing 83 verses). Arched niches inside the portals have verses from Sura-81 entitled 'Izash-Shamso Kuvvirat' (The Folding Up), Sura-82 entitled 'Izas-Samaun Fatarat' (The Cleaving in Sunder), Sura-84 entitled 'Iz-as-Samaun Shaqqat' (The Rending in Sunder) and Sura-98 entitled 'Lam-Yankonil Kafaroo' (The Evidence). In the mortuary hall, around the frieze and arched niches are inscribed verses from Sura-67 entitled 'Mulk' (Dominion), Sura-48 entitled 'Path'

(Victory), Sura-77 entitled 'Mursalat' (Those Sent Forth) and Sura-39 entitled 'Zumar' (The Crowds).

Besides these Quranic verses, Persian inscriptions are found inlaid in between beautiful stylized floral patterns on the tombstones and the cenotaphs in the lower and upper hall respectively. They are epitaphs:

The one's on Mumtaz's cenotaph are: On the south side of Mumtaz's cenotaph (Upper Hall) - "Here lies Arjumand Bano Begum called Mumtaz Mahal who died in 1040 Hijri A.D. 1631)" at the head of the tomb is the line - "He is the everlasting : He is sufficient;" and the following line from the Quran - "God is He, besides whom there is no God. He knoweth what is concealed and what is manifest. He is merciful and compassionate."

On one side of it - "Nearer unto God are those who say 'Our Lord is God.'"

The inscription on the tomb of Shah Jahan is as follows: "The illustrious sculpture and sacred resting place of His Most Exalted Majesty dignified as Razwan (the guardian of Paradise), having his abode in Paradise and his dwelling in the starry heaven, inhabitant of the regions of bliss, Sahib-e-Qiran, Shah Jahan, (which means The Second Lord of Auspicious Conjunction) the king valiant. May his tomb ever flourish and may his abode be in the heavens. He travelled from this transitory world to the world of eternity on the night of the month of Rajab, (1070 A.H.) 1666 A.D."

The tombstones and the cenotaphs also bear a few verses from chapters 40,41,83,2,59,39,3 and 23. They have very carefully been selected for the place and depict the realities of life and death in one way or the other.

CHAPTER 12
Incised Paintings

In this technique, a thin layer of colour pigment (hirmich red earth) is laid over the white (safeda white lead) plaster surface. A floral or conventional design is then drawn on the colour surface, according to which the colour surface is scrapped off, thus exposing the white plaster underneath, now seen only through the scrapped off design. It is thus 'incised painting'. The most developed

stage of this technique is found at the Taj Mahal, in the mosque and its jawab (the rest house), distributed in highly stylised patterns along their whole interiors, from dados to the ceilings. Here again, two colours have been used, a hirmichi red on a white background which is allowed to show magnificently through the scrapped off leaves, flowers and the outlines. The tiny curves of white thus blossom exuberantly on a red ground - portions of the background have thus artistically been brought to the foreground and the foreground recedes into background! Incised.

CHAPTER 13
The Primary Builders of The Taj

Despite several controversies that claim that the Taj Mahal was designed by an Italian Geronimo Veroneo, or a French silversmith Austin de Bordeaux, the first real evidence of the architect's identity emerged in the 1930s when a seventeenth century manuscript called the Diwan-i-Muhand is was found to mention the Taj Mahal. This manuscript contains a collection of several poems written by Luft Allah, including several verses in which he describes his father, Ustad Ahmad from Lahore, as the architect of the Taj Mahal and the Red Fort at Delhi. Ahmad was a Persian engineer-astrologer. Luft Allah also states that Shah Jahan conferred upon his father the title 'Nadir al-Asr' (the Wonder of the Age); unfortunately court histories do not corroborate this claim. Other sources record that Ustad Ahmad was one of the architects of the Red Fort. Further evidence has been found of other large projects undertaken by Ustad Ahmad, strengthening the plausibility of his son's claim. It is interesting to note that Ustad Ahmad had a number of aliases: Ustad Khan

Effendi, Ustad Mohammed, Isa Khan, Isa Effendi and a number of permutations of the name -fictional amalgam of Muslim sounding names, most likely the invention of latter-day British guidebook writers.

It must be emphasised that the design of the Taj Mahal cannot be ascribed to any single mastermind. The Taj is the culmination of an evolutionary process. It is the perfected stage in the development of Mughal architecture. The names of many of the builders who participated in the construction of the Taj in different capacities have come down to us through Persian sources. A project as ambitious as the tomb of Mumtaz Mahal demanded talent from many quarters. From turkey came Ismail Khan a designer of hemispheres and the builder of domes. Qazim Khan, a native of Lahore, travelled to Agra to cast the solid gold finial that crowned the Turkish master's dome.

Chiranjilal, a local lapidary from Delhi was chosen as the chief sculptor and mosaicist. Amanat Khan from Shiraz was the chief calligrapher and this fact is attested on the Taj gateway where his name has been inscribed at the end of the inscription. Muhammad Hamf was the Supervisor of masons, while Mir Abdul Karim and Mukkarimat Khan of Shiraz handled finances and the management of daily production. Sculptors from Bukhara, calligraphers from Syria and Persia, in layets from South India, stonecutters from Baluchistan, a man who specialized in building turrets, another who carved only marble flowers - thirty seven men in all formed the creative nucleus and to this core was added a labour force of twenty thousand workers recruited from across North India.

CHAPTER 14
Materials Used to Build the Taj

Along with the labourers flocking to Agra, materials for construction also began arriving: principally red sandstone from local quarries and marble dug from the hills of far-off Makrana, slightly southwest of Jaipur in Rajasthan. Although the treasury was well filled, such prodigious quantities of rare stuffs were required that caravans travelled to all corners of the empire and beyond in search of precious materials. From Chinese Turkestan in Central Asia came Nephrite jade and crystal; from Tibet - turquoise; from upper Burma - yellow amber; from Badakhshan in the high mountains of northeastern Afghanistan - lapis lazuli; from Egypt - chrysolite; from the Indian Ocean - rare shells, coral and mother-of-pearl. Topazes, onyxes, garnets, sapphires, bloodstone, forty three types of gems in all - ranging in depth from Himalayan quartz to Golconda diamonds - were ultimately to be used in embellishing the Taj Mahal.

In order to transport the marble, a ten mile long ramp of tamped earth was built through Agra and on it trudged an unending parade of elephants and bullock carts dragging blocks of marble to the building site. Once the marble reached the Taj, it was hoisted into place by means of an elaborate post-and-beam pulley manned by teams of mules and masses of workers tugging and hauling.

The first buildings to be constructed were the main tomb and the two mosques that flank it; then came the four minarets; finally the gateway and auxiliary buildings were erected. All were built as integral parts of a single unit, carefully planned to harmonise, for a law of Islam decrees that once a tomb is completed nothing can be added to it and absolutely nothing can ever be taken away from it.

CHAPTER 15
An Overview of The Beauty of The Taj

Besides the miraculous architectural features and the elaborate ornamentation of the Taj Mahal, many additional features, which can often be overlooked, help complement and enhance this spectacular monument.

Background

Unlike other Mughal tombs, the garden of the Taj Mahal has been laid out entirely in front of the tomb and does not play any part in the 'background'. Instead, the background has been provided by the sky. This background is not constant; it changes its colour and texture more than often and the Taj is always presented in a variety of tints and moods. Its shades are subtly reflected on the white marble surface of the Taj Mahal which changes its colour and complexion accordingly.

Marble

The Makrana marble used is of such a nature that it takes on incredibly subtle variations of tint and tone, according to the changes in the light, thus picturing the passing colour of the moment.

Forms and Lines

The composition of the forms and lines of the Taj Mahal is perfectly symmetrical. Here we meet with a beautiful admixture of lines, horizontal with vertical and straight with curved - all harmoniously set together in the total unity. They adopt each other with amazing uniformity. The combination is entirely rhythmic and melodic. Especially the semi-octagonal alcoves at the chamfered angles which are perceptible from every perspective view and give a 3-dimensional appearance from the outset. They emphasise the diagonal lines and suggest depth. Taj is the best example of bilateral symmetry i.e., when it is cut into sections, these are exactly the mirror image of each other.

Solids and Voids

The great depth has also been further suggested by the double arches, one over the other, on each side of the central portal. The solids and voids have very judiciously been distributed to provide a variety, yet an undiminished uniformity. These alcoves, the balconies in each minaret, the chhatris near the dome and certain pronounced projections in each facade allow a beautiful play of light and shadow.

Soaring Effect

The colossal height of the tomb, along with its pyramidal appearance (which is obtained by the receding plinths, the square tomb and the bulbous dome, along with the pilasters surmounted by pinnacles, the tapering minarets and the decreasing volume of the dome culminating in a kalasa) give it a soaring effect. It appears as if it is about to rise into the sky... an ethereal quality full of lightness and grace.

Correction of Illusionary Effects

The indigenous builders of the Taj Mahal fully understood the deceptive nature of the human eye. They knew that the reality and its perception and interpretation thereof differed. The plinth of the main tomb is 2.10" high on an average. But the height varies at different places, particularly the central point between two piers being in each case 0.5" to 0.7" higher than the sides. This convexity has deliberately been given to the plinth in the centre of each arch, or else the building would have appeared as if it were falling down! The facades are not exactly at a right angle with the plinth, but are slightly inclined. The finial is a stupendous crowning feature which measures nearly 10 meters!! The architect fully anticipated the apparent size which a finial would present from such a great height. It has therefore been very ingeniously been planned. These features of construction demonstrate the ability of the Indian architects to reconcile the illusionary effects created by distance and light.

Uniform Size of Calligraphic Characters

The letter of the inscription around archways at the Taj Mahal, are generally supposed to become larger and larger above. On closer scrutiny, however, they are found to be of uniform size. Instead, the letters have been

inscribed densely at the bottom, with little plain surface in between; the inscription becomes more and more sparse as it rises with more plain surface in between the letters. The diminution of the plain surfaces has been accurately calculated. Thus, the optical perspective of the letters has been reconciled and unmistakable uniformity is obtained.

CHAPTER 16
A Look into the World of Mughals

The Mughal Dynasty is a line of Muslim Emperors who reigned in India from 1526 to 1857. Babur, the first Mughal emperor, was a descendant of the Turkish conqueror Timur on his father's side and of the Mongol (in Persian, Mughal) conqueror Genghis Khan on his mother's side, Invaded India from Afghanistan and founded the Mughal Empire on the ruin of the Delhi Sultanate. From 1526, when Babur defeated Sultan Ibrahim Lodi, Mughal Emperors established themselves in neighbouring Agra and Agra Fort remained their main residence, until1638, when Babur's great-great-grandson Shah Jahan built a new capital city in Delhi again. Agra was a repository for all the wealth and talent of one of the most extensive empires in the medieval world.

The many elements that led to the creation of the Taj Mahal had their roots in the reigns of earlier monarchs: 1) Babur 2) Humayun 3) Akbar 4) Jehangir 5) ShahJahan each of whom contributed his particular aesthetic interests and endeavours to the establishment of what we

have subsequently called the Mughal Style, a style which blended the Persian patterns brought by the Mughals with the indigenous genius for fine craftsmanship. However, Shah Jahan's successor and son, Aurangzeb did not have any of the passions for arts and architecture as his father possessed. Only a few monuments in Delhi are associated with Aurangzeb's name.

The amazing achievements in the Mughal architectural tradition owe much to the great talent of Indian artisans and the wealth of material found in India, including the abundance of stone. Each emperor used local materials and indigenous forms and craftsmanship to nurture and bring to fruition a unique enduringly beautiful architectural tradition. The Mughal style found triumphant fulfilment in the building of the Taj Mahal, the most splendid expression of the centuries of Mughal rule in India. The Taj Mahal was the last and greatest architectural flowering of the Mughal period in Agra, before its builder, Shah Jahan shifted the imperial centre of power and administration to what is now called Delhi.

Babur

Although Babur, the founder of the Mughal Empire, ruled only for four brief years, he left his impress on all that was to follow. His love for nature led him to create gardens of great beauty on the formal Charbagh (four quarters) plan. His Arambagh in Agra set the pattern for the gardens which became an intrinsic part of every Mughal fort, palace and tomb in the centuries that followed.

Humayun

Babur's son Humayun succeeded him in 1530, but was defeated by Sher Shah, an Afghan who ruled north India for 15 years, in 1540. Humayun only just managed to regain his father's territories before his death and the accession of his 13 year old son, Akbar, whose 49 year reign laid the foundation of empire and the development of a new style of architecture.

CHAPTER 17
Akbar and Jehangir

Akbar

Humayun's son Akbar, who reigned from 1556 to 1605, decisively defeated the Afghans and firmly established Mughal supremacy in northern India. One of India's greatest rulers, he extended a sound administrative system and won the loyalty of his Hindu subjects by abolishing the personal tax on them and by appointing them to high

civil and military posts. Akbar was receptive to all creeds and doctrines and he tried to found an eclectic religion.

Nine years after he became emperor, Akbar, ordered the construction of a fort beside the river Yamuna in what is now called Agra. The construction proceeded at a hectic pace and within eight years, most of the five hundred buildings within the fort were complete.

By the time he was 26 years old, Akbar had power, prestige and great wealth, but despite a large number of wives, he had no heir. A mystic, by the name of Salim Chisti prophesised that the emperor would have not one but three sons. When the prophesy came true, Akbar decided to build a new capital city (Fatehpur Sikri) on the rocky ridge outside Agra upon which Salim Chisti had his hermitage, using the red sandstone of the ridge itself. Fatehpur Sikri consists of a number of highly individual structures united by the unvarying use of red sandstone and the intricate ornamentation that characterises them. Akbar employed local masons and craftsmen and allowed them the freedom to use their traditional skills to create a style which has been called Akbari.

At the summit of the ridge, Emperor Akbar built an enormous congregational mosque, the Jami Masjid. Later, he added a massive triumphal gate, called the Buland Darwaza at the southern entrance to the mosque. The dominant, aggressive dimensions of the Buland Darwaza provide a perfect foil to the other addition to the mosque;

the single storeyed, daintily decorated tomb built for Salim Chisti.

Akbar's own palace was a double-storeyed structure located behind a pool of water. Spectacular accompanying buildings include the Turkish Sultana Begum's palace, the Diwan-i-khas, the Panch Mahal, the Hawa Mahal, Mariam's palace and Birbal house. The entire palace complex is adorned with exquisite carvings, lattice and pierced stone screens, wall paintings, canopied roofs, carved brackets and pilasters.

Akbar chose the site for his own tomb himself, at a place called Sikandra, near Agra. Sikandra, in a sense, marks the transition between the strong, square, earthbound buildings that characterise the Akbari style and the delicate airy marble structures that Shah Jahan built two generations later. The beginning of inlay work that was so much a part of Shah Jahan's buildings is visible at Sikandra in the bold patterns that decorate the gateway.

Jehangir

Thanks to Akbar's organizing genius, the Mughal administration functioned well under his son Jehangir from 1605 to 1627. There was not a great deal of architectural activity during Jehangir's reign, with one exception. This was the tomb Jehangir and his wife Nur Jahan built for Nur Jahan's father, Itimad-ud-Daulah, who was Jehangir's most important courtier. While the structure itself is fairly simple, the manner in which it has been carved and inlaid with semi-precious stones demonstrates the mastery over this craft which was to find such perfect expression in the Taj Mahal. Lapis lazuli, onyx, jasper, topaz and carnelian have been combined with marble of various hues to create designs of unsurpassed elegance, inter-spread with finely carved screens.

CHAPTER 18
Shah Jahan and Aurangzeb

Shah Jahan

Jehangir's son and successor, Shah Jahan ruled from 1628 to 1658. He was a great patron of the arts and Mughal painting and architecture, blending Persian and Indian traditions, reached their zenith at this time.

With the accession of Shah Jahan to the throne, came a flowering of architecture both in Agra and Delhi. The profusion of white marble buildings raised during the period of Shah Jahan, led one scholar to characterise it as the reign of marble. Red sandstone and brick remained major building materials, but the use of marble is expressive of the very high standards of elegance and luxury that governed all aspects of an architectural project throughout Shah Jahan's reign. The innovations seen in the buildings created during Shah Jahan's reign are striking demonstrations of the effect of particular aesthetic and political concerns. In addition to a greater use of marble, which was a textural quality quite distinct from the red sandstone favoured by his predecessors, there was refinement of the architectural vocabulary. Among specific changes were the introduction of cusped arches and of pillars with tapering shafts and baluster detailing. Many developments can be directly related to a desire to articulate more forcefully paradisiacal and imperial theme, drawing on sources that included European motifs.

Shah Jahan had many earlier structures in the Agra Fort dismantled in order to make room for his own marble pavilions. It seems that immediately upon his accession in 1628, Shah Jahan ordered palace additions to the existing forts at Agra and Lahore. The most notable complex of white marble palace structures is situated on the eastern edge of the fortified walls built by Akbar bordering the Yamuna river. Among these is Muthamman Burj (Jasmine Tower), built at a point where the main north-south wall of the fort takes a turn towards the east. The octagonal room, which offers an exceptional view of the Taj Mahal, is supposed to be the place where Shah Jahan died in 1666. The Muthamman Burj is connected with a series of other marble pavilions forming the east side of a large courtyard that once contained a garden. Only the structure and not the flora survive today. To the north of the palace quarters bordering the garden are additional rooms including the Hall of Private Audience, which is a marble pillared hall decorated with profuse inlay. The Shish Mahal which is located close to the royal apartments, has hundreds of small mirrors embedded in stucco decorations, in intricate floral and geometrical designs. Some distance away is the magnificent Moti Masjid, the Pearl Mosque built at an elevation so that its ethereal domes and kiosks are visible above the walls of the fort.

Aurangzeb

Shah Jahan's son Aurangzeb was the last Great Mughal. Reigning from 1658 to 1707, he was a stern puritan and a religious bigot who sought to impose orthodox Islam on all of India. He dismissed Hindus from public service, re-imposed tax on them and destroyed their temples. Aurangzeb spent the latter half of the reign trying to conquer southern India. Although he brought the Mughal Empire to its greatest extent, his wars helped weld the

Marathas into a powerful enemy and exhausted imperial resources.

Although patronage declined after the reign of Shah Jahan, elaborate architectural projects were undertaken for later Mughal rulers. The Badshahi Mosque in Lahore and the Pearl Mosque in the Delhi fort are but two examples built for Aurangzeb. Aurangzeb chose to be buried in a simple open-air grave, but the tomb of his wife (Bibi-ka-Maqbara) at Aurangabad, is quite elaborate. Although small, the Pearl Mosque in particular, represents a continuation not only of the architectural vocabulary established during the reign of Shah Jahan but also of the use of expensive building materials such as white marble, though the elongated shape of domes and arches signals a change in taste.

Soon after Aurangzeb's death the Mughal empire broke up. The 19th and last Mughal ruler, Bahadur Shah II was deposed by the British in 1858.

CHAPTER 19
The Myths of the Taj

The story of the second Taj

According to popular legend, Shah Jahan decided to construct another Taj Mahal in black marble on the other side of the river Yamuna and to connect the two by a bridge. This structure was intended to be his own tomb. It has been recorded almost contemporarily by Tavernier: "Shah Jahan began to build his own tomb on the other side of the river but the war with his sons interrupted his plan and Aurangzeb who reigns at present is not disposed to complete it." Later gazetteers and guide books mention this story almost invariably. The irregular position of the cenotaph of Shah Jahan as compared to that of Mumtaz.

Mahal which occupies the exact centre of the hall is said to be proof of this assumption. The Mehtab Burj and the wall adjoining it opposite the Taj Mahal are generally said to be the foundations and remains of the proposed plan.

Many scholars, however, believe that this idea belongs to fiction rather than history. The traces which are identified as the foundations of the second Taj are actually the enclosing wall of a garden founded by Babur. The irregular position of Shah Jahan's cenotaph in comparison to Mumtaz Mahal's, is similar to that at the tomb of Itmad-ud-Daulah and thus should not be of any striking significance. Besides, according to Islamic law, bodies are buried with their faces towards Macca and legs towards the south and the husband is placed on the right hand side of his wife. The interpretation that the cenotaph of Shah Jahan was not meant to be placed here appears to be superfluous.

The Taj is Sinking

The architect of the Taj Mahal aimed at giving maximum strength and stability to the tomb and worked out the minutest details with utmost precision: the weight of the entire structure is uniformly distributed, extraordinarily massive piers and vaults were constructed to support this heavy load, the very best quality of bonding material helped combat the disrupted tensile stress etc. However, in spite of all these precautions and care, dangerous cracks and leakages developed in the substructure just four years after its completion. Aurangzeb in his letter to Shah Jahan in 1652 mentions these cracks. Some defects were discovered about the same time in the dome. Though thorough repairs were undertaken, the nature of the cracks was not discovered. The cracks were again noticed to have developed to dangerous proportions in 1810. As a result an Advisory Committee on the restoration and conservation of the monument was set up and a survey with reference to the damage was undertaken.

Some very important facts resulted from this survey. It was discovered that the plinth of the mausoleum on the northern side (or the riverside) is lower than on the south by 3.5 cms. Cracks were not noticed on the exterior wall, but they were definitely present on the second storey vaults of the marble structure and, on a much larger scale, in the underground vaults below the northern side. The long series of cracks in the underground vaults may be due to the crushing of lime on account of the excessive weight, or as seems more probable, this may be due to the sinking of the whole structure towards the riverside!! Such a sinking would shift the load out of balance slowly and gradually and the unequal settlement would crack the weak points, particularly the soffits of the vaults and arches, which is actually happening in the underground chambers. A structure which stands on the edge of water has a natural tendency to move towards the more open side, the higher edge always acting as a strong buttress, thrusting it in the opposite direction. It is the whole mass and not a part of it that is gradually sinking. This is what can justifiably be concluded from the available data. Many experts and activists have shown concern and fear that depletion of river Yamuna is the root cause of this sinking which is further causing cracks in the structure.

CHAPTER 20
More Interesting Myths

The Taj was designed by an Italian architect

Some European scholars held the view that the Taj was designed by an Italian - Geronimo Veroneo. This was first suggested by Father Manrique, an Augustinian Friar, who came to Agra in 1640 A.D., to secure the release of Father Antony who had been imprisoned by the Mughals. It was in Lahore that he met Father Joseph de Castro, the executor of Veroneo who died at Lahore in 1640 A.D. and it was Castro who told him about 'the Venetian by the name Geronimo Veroneo who came in the Portuguese ships and died in the city of Lahore before he reached it...'

During the reign of Jehangir, a goldsmith named Veroneo did in fact come to India and, as mentioned by Father Manrique, did die on his way to Lahore. He lived for a time in Agra and prospered there. He knew many influential Europeans throughout the North Indian provinces and when he died, he was buried in the Christian cemetery of Padres Santos in Agra.

The theory that Veroneo designed the Taj is intriguing and still finds occasional champions, especially in Italy. But the scales of evidence weigh heavily against it. True there is the testimony of Father Manrique, but he was no more than a casual tourist who heard that the Taj had been built by an Italian. However, nowhere else is mention made of Veroneo's participation in planning the Taj Mahal. As a matter of fact, there is no record that Veroneo had any skill other than that of working with gold. Other Europeans who saw the Taj under construction never mentioned his name and furthermore, it is difficult to suppose that an artist trained in seventeenth century Italy, the Italy of Bernini, could build a mausoleum that would typify Indo-Persian architecture. The Taj is not an isolated phenomenon, the creation of a single mastermind but the glorious consummation of a great epoch of art.

The basement chambers and a probable third grave

Two staircases on the northern side of the red sandstone plinth of the Taj lead below into the basement chambers which are seventeen in number and have been laid out in a line on the riverside of a narrow through-corridor. The rooms and corridor are of arcuate construction in brick and plaster, with stucco and painting ornamentation, distributed aesthetically on the soffits. At the extreme points on both sides there are doors sunk in the northern wall. They were blocked up permanently and securely with thick masonry at some unknown date, undoubtedly for some well calculated purpose. As may be surmised, the set on the northern side could have been repeated on the sides below the marble structure, with a rotating corridor, chambers and probably a crypt in the centre - all being interconnected.

This crypt would have contained the third and the real set of graves. The custom of providing cenotaphs or replicas had been followed by the Turks and the Mughals alike as we meet with this practice at the tomb of Iltutmish at Delhi and at the tombs of Saqid Khan and Akbar at Agra. The tomb of Akbar has three tombstones, one on the grave and two as cenotaphs. The tomb of Itmad-ud-Dauhlah and Chini-ka-Rauza too had three tombstones each. The lowest of the former was contained in a crypt which was originally accessible from the riverside and has now been completely blocked up. These examples indicate that the Mughals liked to provide three tombstones in a mausoleum. At the Taj, the third is traditionally claimed to exist. It is only in these underground vaults that the third set could have been placed. The doors in the basement corridor no doubt exist and must have originally given entry to some underground arrangement of chambers and corridors. Though they are now impregnably blocked, their existence lends weight to the legendary version.

CHAPTER 21
Taj Mahal - A True Wonder

The Archaeological Survey of India has decided that Taj Mahal will remain closed on Fridays for the public except for those who go for afternoon prayers in the mosque next to the 17th century monument. The monument, which attracts thousands of visitors every day, previously remained closed on Mondays.

The Taj remains open from 6 a.m-7 p.m everyday except Fridays. Entry fee for foreign tourists is Rs. 1000/-and Rs. 40/-for Indians. For tourists from SAARC and BIMSTEC countries the entry fee is Rs. 530/-. On Fridays, people will be allowed to go for the customary prayers between 12:00 hrs 14:00 hrs at the mosque in the Taj Mahal complex.

Described by the Indian classical poet Tagore as a 'tear on the face of eternity', the Taj Mahal is undoubtedly the zenith of Mughal architecture and quite simply one of the world's most marvelous buildings. Volumes have been written on its perfection and its image adorns countless glossy brochures and guide books; nonetheless, the reality never fails to overwhelm all who see it and few words can do it justice.

Play of Light

The glory of the monument is strangely undiminished by the crowds of tourists who visit each day, as small and insignificant as ants in the face of this immense and captivating monument. That said, the Taj is at its most alluring in the relative quiet of early morning, shrouded in mists and bathed with a soft red glow. As its vast marble surfaces fall into shadow or reflect the sun, its colour changes, from soft grey and yellow to pearly cream and dazzling white; it's well worth visiting at different times. This play of light is an important decorative device, symbolically implying the presence of Allah, who is never represented in anthropomorphic form.

CHAPTER 22
Sayings on Taj

From studied awe to sheer ecstasy, people have literally competed to say the most beautiful things about the Taj Mahal. Some have admired its beauty; others have revealed the various activities that took place here.

Shah Jahan's own composition in praise of the Tajis found in Badshah Nama: "...The sight of this mansion creates sorrowing sighs and makes sun and moon shed tears from their eyes. In this world this edifice has been made to display thereby the Creator's glory."

From the Travels in the Moghul Empire, 1670 by the French traveller Bernier: "The Quran is continually read with apparent devotion by certain Mullahs kept in the Mausoleum for that purpose... It is opened with much ceremony once a year.. and no Christian is admitted within, lest its sanctity be profaned."

In 1783 the British painter Hodges says of the tomb: "It appears like a perfect pearl on an azure ground. The effect is such I have never experienced from any work of art."

By the time of the British conquest of India, the attitude to the Taj had changed. The beautiful memorial had turned into a pleasure resort; in its gardens, Englishman met their lovers. On its terrace they danced while the mosque and the jawab were rented out to honeymooners!

Writes the then well-known British officer, Colonel Sleeman's wife: "I cannot tell, what I think. I do not know how to criticise such a building but I can tell what I feel. I would die tomorrow to have such another over me."

CHAPTER 23
In and Around The Taj

Visiting Agra is not just restricted to paying a visit to the Taj Mahal! There are numerous other monumental site and forts that may have taken a backseat because of the crowning glory of the Taj Mahal, but are nevertheless worth visit for their architectural magnificence and historical significance.

One can visit Agra Fort, Itmad-ud-dualah's Tomb, Rambagh, Dayal Bagh and Jama Masjid are some noteworthy monument sites of Agra that remind the visitors about the legacy that Mughal's left behind.

Agra fort

Built principally as a military establishment by Akbar in 1565, the red sandstone Agra fort was partially converted into a palace during Shah Jahan's time. Though the principal structure was built by Akbar, many more additions were made by his grandsons. This massive fort is 2.5 kms long and is considered as the predecessor of the Delhi Red fort. The colossal walls are 20 feet high and the whole fort is encircled by a fend moat. Amar Singh

gate towards the south is the only entry point in the fort. The building and structures inside the fort gives an impression of a city within the city. Many of the building inside the fort are now closed for the public. The marble pearl mosque inside the fort is one of the most stunningly beautiful mosques in India.

Diwan-e-Am: This structure was originally made out of wood but was later constructed in the present form by Shah Jahan. The throne room bears a clear influence of Shah Jahan's style with the inlaid carvings and panels of marble with floral motifs. This hall of public hearing is the place where the Emperor heard the petitions of the public and met the officials. The hall of public hearing gives way to the Nagina Mosque and the Ladies bazar where only lady merchants were allowed to sell items to the Mughal ladies.

Diwan-e-Khas: This was the hall of private audience. This hall was also added by Shah Jahan. This hall is divided into two rooms connected by three arches and it was here that the famous peacock throne was kept before being shifted to Delhi by Aurangzeb and finally carried away to Iran.

Octagonal Tower: This exquisitely carved tower is close to the Diwan-e-Khas. It was here that Shah Jahan spent last seven years of his life imprisoned by his son Aurangzeb. The tower was considered to provide one of the best views of the Taj but today the pollution has reduced the visibility. The tower is in bad shape today but blank spaces and the empty inlay works give an idea how this building must have looked in those days.

Jehangir Palace: This was built by Akbar for his favorite son Jehangir to provide him with the comfort and luxury inside the fort.

Mina Masjid: Just above the Sheesh Mahal is situated the Mina Masjid, which is believed to be constructed by Shah Jahan for strictly private use. The Mina Masjid is enclosed on all the four sides by high walls. The marble mosque has three small arches in its facade, which are plain and unadorned.

Moti Masjid: Moti Masjid is situated to the right of Diwan-E-Aam of the Agra Fort. One can see the domes of the Moti Masjid, which is the prettiest of all the buildings at Agra Fort. Moti Masjid is a white marble structure

built by Shah Jahan for his family members and court chiefs. Moti Masjid made out of white marble is one of the ancient mosques situated in Agra. It used to shine like a pearl once upon a time and hence the name.

Machhi Bhawan: Opposite to the Diwan-e-Khas is the machhi bhawan, the fish enclosure. The emperor sat on the white marble platform facing the enclosure. It once contained pools and marble fountains, which were carried off by the Jat Raja Suraj Mal to his palace at Deeg.

Sheesh Mahal: Opposite to the Musamman Burj and just below the Diwan-E-Khas hall is the Sheesh Mahal or the glass palace. It is believed to have been the harem dressing room and its walls are inlaid with tiny mirrors, which are the best specimens of glass mosaic decoration in India.

Jahangiri Mahal: This is the first notable building inside the Agra Fort. It was built by Akbar as women's quarters and is the only building that survives among his original! palace buildings. It is built of stone and is simply decorated in the exterior. This elegant, double storeyed building reflects a strong Hindu influence with protruding balconies and domed chhatris.

Anguri Bagh: These formal 85 square geometric gardens lie to the left of the fort. During Shah Jahan's time, the beauty of the gardens was considerably enhanced by decorative flower beds.

Golden Pavilions: The curved chala roofs of the small pavilions by the Khaas Mahal are based on the roof shape of Bengali village huts constructed out of curved bamboo, designed to keep off heavy rains. The shape was first expressed in stone by the sultans of Bengal. Theses pavilions are traditionally associated with Shah Jahan's daughters: Roshnara and Jahannara Begum.

Musamman Burj: On the left of the Khaas Mahal is the Musamman Burj built by Shah Jahan. It is a beautiful octagonal tower with an open pavilion standing close to the Shah Jahan's private hall Dewan-e-khas. With its openness, elevation and the benefit of cool evening breezes flowing in off the Yamuna River, it is also considered to have the most poignant view of the Taj Mahal. It is here that Shah Jahan spent his last few years as a captive of his son Aurangazeb and Shah Jahan lay on his death bed, gazing at Taj Mahal.

Fatehpur Sikri

37 kms from Agra is built a city pre-dominantly in Red Sandstone and is called Fatehpur Sikri. This town was built by the Mughal Emperor, Akbar. He had planned this city as his capital but shortage of water compelled him to abandon the city. After this within 20 years, the capital of Mughals was shifted to Lahore.

Fatehpur Sikri was built during 1571 and 1585. Today this ghost city has a population of about 30,000. This deserted city has retained many of the old structures, because of the efforts of the Archaeological department.

Fatehpur Sikri is one of the finest examples of Mughal architectural splendour at its height. Though the city is in ruins, it is a place to visit if one comes to Agra. But in real terms Fatehpur Sikri is a place where one should spend some time. The sunset over the ruins is sight to cherish.

Fatehpur Sikri is the best example of the culmination of Hindu and Muslim architecture. Fatehpur Sikri Mosque is said to be a copy of the mosque in Mecca and has designs, derived from the Persian & Hindu architecture.

Diwan-khana-I-khaas: To the right is an apparently looking two storeyed building, with corner kiosks, known as Diwan-khana-I-khaas or Hall Of Private Audience. On entering it, one finds only a single vaulted chamber. In the centre stands a profusely carved column supporting a colossal-bracketed capital. Four narrow causeways project from the centre and run to each corner of the chamber. It is believed that Akbar's throne occupied the circular space over the capital and the corners were assigned to the four ministers, Diwan-e-khas-fateh-pur-sikri.

Diwan-I-Am: The journey to the royal palace begins with Diwan-I-Am or the Hall Of Public Audience. This hall was also used for celebrations and public prayers. It has cloisters on three sides of a rectangular courtyard. To the west is a pavilion with the Emperor's throne. Beautiful jali screen on either side separated the ladies attending the court.

The Treasury: To the left of the Diwan-I-Khaas is the Treasury or Ankh Michauli, once believed to have been used for playing the game, comprising three rooms each protected by a narrow corridor which were manned by guards.

Turkish Sultana's House: To the left of the Pachisi Board is the Turkish Sultana's house. The house, as its location at the corner of Anup Talao shows, was a pavilion for repose, attached to the pool. The geometrical pattern on the ceiling is reminiscent of Central Asian carvings in wood.

Palace of Jodha Bai: To the left of the Sunehra Makanis the largest and the most important building in the royal palace, named after Akbar's Rajput wife, Jodha Bai. This spacious palace was assured of privacy and security by high walls and a 9 metre guarded gate to the east. The architecture is a blend of styles with Hindu columns and Muslim cupolas.

Daulatkhana-I-khas: Located in the corner to the left is the emperor's private chamber. It has two main rooms on the ground floor. One housed Akbar's library while the larger room was his resting area. On the first floor is the Khwabgah or the bed-chamber. It was connected with the Turkish Sultana's house, the Panch Mahal, Mariam's House and the Jodha Bai's palace by corridors.

Sunehra Makan: Opposite to the Diwan-i-Khas is the palace of Akbar's Rajput wife, Mariam-Uz-Zamani. This two-storeyed building is richly adorned by gold murals in Persian style. The beams have inscriptions of verses by Akbar's brother, Faizi.

Panch Mahal: To the right of Sunehra Makan is the elegant, airy 5 storeyed pavilion, the Panch Mahal. Each floor over here is smaller than the one below and it rises to a single domed kiosk on top supported by four columns providing a magnificent view of the city and its environs.

Hawa Mahal And Nagina Masjid: To the right of Jodha Bai's palace is Hawa Mahal, the Palace of Winds. This small-screened wind tower faces the garden and is attached to the palace. The garden is laid out in the Char Bagh style with straight walls intersecting at right angles and divided by shallow channels.

Birbal's Palace: To the north west of the Jodha Bai's Palace is the 2 storeyed palace occupied by Akbar's two senior queens - Ruqaiya Sultan Begum and Salima Sultan Begum. It is a two storeyed structure-four rooms and two porches with pyramidal roofs below and two rooms with cupolas and screened terraces above. The building combines Hindu and Muslim styles of architecture.

The Jami Masjid: One of the largest mosques in India, Jami Masjid was built in 1571 AD. Inside, there is a vast congregational courtyard. To the right, at the corner, is the Jammat Khana Hall and next to this is the tomb of the royal ladies. To the left of the Jami Masjid is the Stone Cutters' mosque, the oldest place of worship at Fatehpur Sikri. It is entered through the eastern entrance known as the Buland Darwaza.

Dargah Of Sheikh Salim Chisti: To the North of the Mosque is the Dargah of Shaikh Salim Chishti. The construction of this Dargah commenced in 1571 and took couple of years to complete. Here, childless women come for blessings of the saint. Even Akbar was blessed with three sons, when he came here. The lattice work in the Dargah is among the finest to be found anywhere in India.

Buland Darwaza: This gate can be approached from the outside by a 13-metre flight of steps which adds to its grandeur. The gate erected in 1602 AD to commemorate Akbar's victory over Deccan is the highest and grandest gateway in India and ranks among the biggest in the world.